LET'S HAVE CHURCH
In a Book

"ARE YOU A USEABLE VESSEL?"
"2 CORINTHIANS 4:7"

DONYALE M. DABNEY

Let's Have Church In A Book
Are You A Usaeble Vessel?
Copyright © 2021 by Donyale M. Dabney

Christian, Religious

Library of Congress Control Number: 2021909861
ISBN-13:   Paperback: 978-1-64749-468-1
              ePub: 978-1-64749-469-8

All rights reserved. No part of this publication may be reproduced, distributed, or transmitted in any form or by any means, including photocopying, recording, or other electronic or mechanical methods, without the prior written permission of the publisher or author, except in the case of brief quotations embodied in critical reviews and certain other noncommercial uses permitted by copyright law.

Although every precaution has been taken to verify the accuracy of the information contained herein, the author and publisher assume no responsibility for any errors or omissions. No liability is assumed for damages that may result from the use of information contained within.

Printed in the United States of America

GoToPublish LLC
1-888-337-1724
www.gotopublish.com
info@gotopublish.com

Contents/Order of Service

My Journey to Destiny v
Introduction: Let's Have Church 1
Praise/Worship (Exhortation) 3
Praise/Worship ("Let us Sing.") 9
Praise/Worship ("Let us Dance.") 19
Praise/Worship ("Let Us Worship") 24
My personal prayer 33
Word of The Lord: Setting our foundation 35
Word of The Lord: "Are you a useable vessel?" 51
Pride 62
Pride in the Church 78
Deliverance From Pride 86
Rejection 93
Altar Call 109
Study Notes 114
Acknowledgements 121
About The Author 123
Other Books Written By Author 127

My Journey to Destiny

(Acknowledgements) to my first spiritual father: To Bishop Kenneth C. Ulmer:

I would first like to thank you for depositing within me what it means to worship. The bible says, *they that worship must worship in spirit and truth.* The ministry that God has given to you touches the very core of the heart. You are not just a teacher, but you are a true worshipper, and that is why the spirit of the Lord rests and resides in your church. Where God is being worshipped is where He will be. I believe your doors will always overflow with people because God is truly being worshipped there. Jesus said, "if I am lifted up, I will draw all men to me." So, keep doing what you are doing, exalting the one and only true living God. God's hands will always be resting on you.

In addition to me learning about worship, you have also taught me how to dream big. You have always said that we do not serve a small God, so we should not have small dreams. You said that we serve a BIG God, so we should have BIG dreams. You are, in fact, a visionary whom God has anointed to encourage people to step up and reach for the stars. I appreciate the impartation that I have received from your ministry, and I pray that God's blessing will continue to overtake you… 😊

Introduction

What is "Let's Have Church" in a book? Well, let's just say it is exactly what it sounds like. We are having church service in a book. This book series is designed to reach those people who have not been able for whatever reason to attend a church service. Don't get me wrong. My goal is not to deter anyone from assembling themselves to a local church body, so pastors, please don't boycott me just yet. But through the leading of the Holy Ghost, I am making sure that everyone is given an opportunity to hear the word. I am taking the word to them. I am making the word available for those who are incarcerated; those in the hospital; and those who simply work all the time. I remember when I was pregnant with my 2nd child; I was hospitalized, and

I was put on bed rest for two and a half months. During this time, I was miserable. Not only was I miserable because I lost my sense of independence, but I was equally miserable because I was not able to attend church. I know I had my TV, but it wasn't church. I know I had my CD's, but it wasn't church. I needed to hear a word. I needed to be taught the word. "Let's Have Church" in a book is designed to do just that. Believers will be given an opportunity to hear a word that is relevant, personal, and prophetic, a word that can be applied to their lives that will ultimately encourage them to grow and come up to another level. Not only would believers benefit from this series, but non-believers will also be given the opportunity to accept Christ as their personal Savior. Hallelujah! So, women put on your big hats, men put on your finest suits, close your eyes, turn on your sanctified imagination… and "Let's Have Church!" (in a book of course ☺)

Praise/Worship

Exhortation

Father God, in the name of Jesus, we come to thank you. We thank You, Father, for who You are in our lives. Lord, we realize that You did not have to allow us to be here, but You chose us as Your very elect, and for that alone, we thank You, Father. We could be sleeping in our grave, but by Your grace and Your mercy, we have yet another day to offer up our praise and thanksgiving unto You. Father, we thank You for the precious blood. We know that had it not been for You giving Your Son to die on the cross for our sins, we would be lost. Thank You for redeeming us back from the hands of the enemy. Thank You for Your tender mercies and immeasurable favor.

Thank You, Jesus, for going down into the bowels of hell and taking victory over death and the grave. Thank You for taking back the keys to the kingdom and making it available unto us so that we may not only have life but have it more abundantly. Thank You, Father, that we have been given the victory. Hallelujah! The bible says we are to enter into His gates with thanksgiving and enter into His courts with Praise. We are to be thankful unto Him and bless His Holy name.

Father God, we praise You for being who You are. You are the King of Glory; The Lord God who is strong and mighty; the Lord God who is mighty in battle. We will forever bless your Holy name. Lord God, we lift You up today high above the earth, and we elevate Your greatness. We praise You for Your marvelous splendor and the glorious majesty of Your kingdom. Your kingdom is everlasting, and Your dominion endures throughout all generations. Lord, we rejoice in Your goodness. We celebrate Your awesomeness. Truly, You are worthy to be praised. You are holy, unchanging, forgiving, unconditionally loving. You are worthy, Lord, of all our praises. You are awesome; magnificent; remarkable; amazing. Yes, You are worthy of being praised. Lord

God, we extol thee; we honor thee; we exalt thee; we magnify thee because You are truly worthy to be praised!

> *"Let everything that has breath, praise the Lord.*
> *Praise the Lord."*
> *(Psalm 150:6)*

It says in His word that we must praise Him, exalt Him, and extol Him forever and ever.

God has been so good to us. Who are we not to honor Him? He woke us up this morning. He protects our children. He is responsible for us getting that promotion on our job. You mean to tell me we cannot praise Him? He is gracious. He is compassionate. He is slow in anger and rich in love. We should celebrate Him.

He is so faithful. Who are we not to be faithful to Him? He is dependable and faithful in all his promises.

He has never made a promise that He did not keep. That is what I mean when I say He is dependable. How many people can you truly say you can depend on?

Ok, that number is great, but let me re-phrase the question. How many people can you truly say you can depend on when you are acting like a fool? Uh-huh, I bet that number reduced to one, and I hope that one is God.

God loves us even when we do not deserve to be loved. God deserves all our praises.

He deserves all our attention, our love, our time, and our emotion. He loves us. Who are we not to love Him? God is amazing. Well, let us tell Him, sing it to Him, and express it. We should speak praise, sing praise, and praise the Lord in the dance. With all that we have, we should praise the Lord.

Speak praise aloud!

> *"I shout for joy to the Lord, all the earth,"*
> *(Psalm 100)*

In your heart!

> *"Glory in His holy name;*
> *let the hearts of those who seek the lord rejoice."*
> *(Psalm 105:3)*

In your spirit, and in your soul! God expects us to let worship flow out of our spirits and give Him praise from our souls. He has done too much for us to hold back. Why should we be ashamed and worry about who is sitting next to or in front of us?

They don't know how good God has been to us. God is a wonderful God, a glorious God, a deserving God, and a God worthy to be praised. Why should we be concerned with what we look like to others? God wasn't concerned about how He looked when He stepped in and pulled us out of our mess. So, let us step outside of our comfort zones and reach down into the depth of our souls and, with all that we have, give the praise that the almighty God deserves.

> *"Clap your hands, all you nations;*
> *shout to God with cries of joy."*
> ***(Psalm 47:1)***

My mouth will speak in praise of the Lord. Let every creature praise His holy name forever and ever.

Let's enter His gates with thanksgiving and His courts with praise. Lord God, we first come before you giving you all the thanks. You have been so good to us. You have kept us in our right minds, you have protected our homes, you have covered our lives, and we thank you. We are truly grateful for what you have done, what you are doing, and what you are going to do in our lives. Lord God, you are rich in love and full of grace, and for that alone, we thank you. We offer up thanksgiving and praise because you are great and greatly to be praised.

> *"It is good to give thanks to the Lord.*
> *And to sing praises to your name, Oh Most High."*
> *(Psalms 92:1)*

Praise/Worship

"Let us Sing."

IT IS GOOD TO GIVE THANKS *(Psalms 92)*
By Donyale Dabney

Verse 1

It is good to give thanks to the Lord

It is good to give thanks to the Lord

And the Sing praises to thy name Oh Most High

It is good to give thanks to the Lord

Verse 2

To declare thy loving kindness in the morning

To declare thy loving kindness in the morning

And thy faithfulness by night by night

It is good to give thanks to the Lord

Repeat verses.

(Bridge)

The Lord He rules He Reigns

He is clothed with majesty

He's the King of all Kings and the Lord of all Lords.

It is good to give thanks to the Lord

Repeat bridge.

It is good to give thanks to the Lord

It is good to give thanks to the Lord

It is good to give thanks to the Lord

It is good to give thanks to the Lord

Psalm 150

1 Praise the Lord.

Praise God in his sanctuary;

Praise him in his mighty heavens.

2 Praise him for his acts of power;

praise him for his surpassing greatness.

3 Praise him with the sounding of the trumpet,

praise him with the harp and lyre,

4 Praise him with tambourine and dancing,

praise him with the strings and flute,

5 Praise him with the clash of cymbals,

praise him with resounding cymbals.

6 Let everything that has breath, praise the Lord.

Psalm 149:1

1 *Praise the Lord.*
Sing to the Lord a new song,
His praise in the assembly of the saints.

HE'S BEEN SO GOOD TO ME
By Donyale Dabney

Verse 1

At first

Donyale M. Dabney

Things weren't right with me.

I was headed for destruction

And I could not see

Then my

God took me by the hand

And he turned my life around

He gave me peace and happiness

(Chorus)

He's been so good to me

He came into my life

He opened my eyes and showed me

What love was supposed to be

He's been so good to me

I gotta thank the Lord

I gotta praise him just for blessing me.

Verse2

When I

Fell down

He was right there

To pick me up and placed my feet

Back on solid ground

Never

Has he left me alone

He's always been right by my side

That is why I love him so

(Chorus)

He's been so good to me

He came into my life

He opened my eyes and showed me

What love was supposed to be

He's been so good to me

I gotta thank the Lord

I gotta praise him just for blessing me.

(Bridge)

He's been so good

He's been so good

So good to me

He's been so good

He's been so good

God has been so good to me

(Chorus)

He's been so good to me

He came into my life

He opened my eyes and showed me

What love was supposed to be

He's been so good to me

I gotta thank the Lord.

I gotta praise him just for blessing me.

Let us exhort the Lord!

The Bible tells us to praise the Lord. The Lord has been so good to us. He wakes us every morning; He shows us a brand-new day, a day we have never seen before, a day with brand new mercies.

God is so good and *His mercy endureth forever.*

We have to give Him praise!

He has covered and protected us from all hurt, harm and dangers, both seen and unseen.

Let us lift up His Holy Name!

Bless His Holy Name!

Bless that wonderful name of Jesus!

He has been so good!

He has been so merciful.

His loving-kindness is everlasting.

Oh, Let's magnify Him.

Let us exalt Him!

He's been so good let's Praise Him! Come on, Zion!

Let's Praise the Lord.

Praise ye the Lord.

PRAISE YE THE LORD
By Donyale Dabney

(Chorus)

Praise ye the Lord

Who's the light of my life

Praise ye the Lord

Who gives me rest

On sleepless nights

Donyale M. Dabney

He has done so many things

For me

For me

Praise ye the Lord

Who'll always be my everything

Verse 1

Lord, I lift up my voice

I give you all the praise

All the glory

All the thanks

Just for saving me

Father, I didn't deserve a thing

A life so full of shame

But you sent your son

To die for me

And now my life has changed

Now I'm singing

(Chorus)

Praise ye the Lord

Who's the light of my life

Praise ye the Lord

Who gives me rest

On sleepless nights

He has done so many things

For me

For me

Praise ye the Lord

Who'll always be my everything

Verse 2

Lord, I offer you my life

And surrender my all to you

Take over me

And have your way

I'm available to be used

Father, no one really knows

Just where you brought me from

Where would I be

Without your Grace

Without your mercy

Donyale M. Dabney

Now I'm singing

(Chorus)

Praise ye the Lord

Who's the light of my life

Praise ye the Lord

Who gives me rest

On sleepless nights

He has done so many things

For me

For me

Praise ye the Lord

Who'll always be my everything

(Bridge)

Praise Him, Praise Him Praise Him

Praise, Praise, ye the Lord

Praise Him, Praise Him, Praise Him

Praise, Praise, ye the Lord

(Chorus)

Praise/Worship

"Let us Dance."

Psalm 149:3

"Let them praise his name in the dance."

Theme: Being connected to the vine.

"I am the vine, you are the branches, He who abides in Me and I in Him bears much fruit for without Me you can do nothing."
(John 15:5)

"Song: I need you now." by Smokie Norful

Purpose: To show the advantages of being connected and the consequences of being disconnected.

Cast:

7 dancers in total

1 person as Jesus

3 people as branches

1 worldly female teen

2 worldly males

Attire:

Jesus - dressed in all white with a crown on his head

Branches - dressed in regular blue jeans and oversized white t-shirts with vines drawn on them and leaves glued to them.

Worldly female teen – dressed like a grown-up woman

2 Worldly males - dressed hip-hop with cell phones

Description of choreography:

The choreography opens with the 3 branches (dancers) dancing around Jesus. The purpose is to show the branches (dancers) being in harmony and in sync with being connected to Jesus. The dance moves will show the branches dancing with Jesus, bowing down, praying, worshipping, praising Him and reading the word.

Props: Bibles, tambourines (praising)

Emotion: Happy, smiling

While dancing with Jesus, one of the branches (dancers) manages to get disconnected from Him. The dancer, (preferably a female), gets angry and frustrated and starts to rebel. She looks down at her attire and tears off the leaves on her t-shirt, running away from Jesus to the other side of the room. While the other two branches (dancers) are still connected to Jesus doing the same dance movements, the audience's attention should now be focused on the rebellious branch (dancer).

While she is on the other side of the room away from Jesus, she ties up her t-shirt to one side, pulls out her lipstick and mirror, and begins to apply her make-up. Then she hooks up with the worldly female teen, and they both notice two guys and wave to get their attention. The rebellious branch (dancer) goes over to worldly male #1 to talk to him. He pulls out his cell phone and begins to talk on it. Then he rejects her by brushing her off and walking away. Then she walks up to worldly male # 2, and he pulls out his cell phone and begins texting. He whispers in her ear, and she blushes and shakes her head. He rejects her and walks away. Then she turns around and goes back over to the worldly female teen, and she uses the gesture *talk to the hand* and walks away. The rebellious dancer, feeling rejected, falls to her knees, puts her face in her hands, and begins to cry. She throws a tantrum by crying, pulling her hair, and beating on the ground.

At this moment, the dancer shows a lot of emotion. (Fear, frustration, anger, shame, hurt.) After throwing her tantrum, she looks at the cross she is wearing around her neck, looks to the sky and remembers Jesus. Then she looks over to the other side of the room where the other two branches are still connected and dancing with Jesus. She proceeds to crawl back. Jesus stops, turns to look at the rebellious branch, and stretches his hand out. She falls on her face in repentance. Jesus takes her by the hand, lifts her up, puts her in position, and she is reconnected. She starts dancing, praising, and worshipping again.

Emotion: Smiling, happy

(Praise God!)

Hallelujah!

"I will seek what was lost and bring back what was driven away, bind up the broken and strengthen what was sick...."

(Ezekiel 34:16) (A)- portion

...... *"But while he was still a long way off, his father saw him and was filled with compassion for him, he ran to his son, threw his arms around him and kissed him. (v21) The son said to him, Father, I have sinned against heaven and against you. I am no longer worthy to be called your son! (v22) "But the father said to his servants, "Quick! Bring the best robe and put it on him. Put a ring on his finger and sandals on his feet. (v23) Bring the fattened calf and kill it. Let's have a feast and celebrate. (v24) or this son of mine was dead and is alive again, he was lost and is found. So, they began to celebrate."*

(Luke 15:20-24).

Praise/Worship

"Let Us Worship"

It is important that we, as believers, worship the Lord. To worship is to reverence; to Glorify; to bow down in adoration; to respect.

When we worship, we are not only worshipping God with our mouths through song or our bodies through dance, but we are worshipping Him with our entire being. Worshipping God is honoring Him with everything that we have; our money; our time; and even our lifestyles. God wants us to acknowledge Him in all that we do. Not out of obligation, but out of pure appreciation of who He is and because we truly love Him.

Jesus states in John 4:24 *that true worshippers must worship the father in spirit and in truth*. Worshipping in *spirit and truth* describes both the **mode** and the **manner** of worship. The **mode**- being the approach or way to worship which should be done in *spirit* and the **manner**- being the conduct or behavior which should be done in *truth*. What does this mean? Well, it basically means that true worship takes place when the spirit of a man or a woman communes with the spirit of God. We are relating to God when we are in spirit (**mode**). According to the word, God is a spirit, so He can only communicate with us through our spirits. We cannot relate to God through our flesh. That is why worshipping God is a spiritual thing. It is not entertainment. It is a time we use to directly connect with our Father and communicate with Him.

True worship also takes place when it is done in all sincerity from our hearts. For us to be truly sincere in our worship of God, our behavior, conduct, and lifestyles must line up with the truth of His word (**manner**). What does this mean? Well, it means that God does not only want us to worship Him in prayer, song, and dance, but God expects us to worship Him with our lives. Only when our lives line up with the truth of His word are we able to sincerely worship from our hearts, and it is from that point our worship is no longer a stench but is a purified worship that is likened to a sweet-smelling aroma unto the Lord.

The Bible tells us in Jeremiah 17:10 *that the Lord searches the heart,* so when we commune with Him, we should do it from the place He searches. Isaiah 29:13 speaks of worshipping not being done from the heart. God says.

"For as much as this people draw near me with their mouth, and with their lips do honor me, but have removed their heart far from me, and their fear toward me is taught by the precept of man." (KJV)

1 Samuel 16:7 says,

"For the Lord seeth not as man seeth; for man looketh on the outward appearance, but the Lord looketh on the heart." (KJV)

So, when we worship, we should speak directly to the Lord with a sincere heart. Tell Him what He means to us. What He's been to us. We don't have to wait until Sunday morning to worship

Him. We can worship Him right now. Let's just close our eyes and think about the goodness of the Lord. Think about how wonderful He is. How good He's been.

Think about all His blessings. If you feel like crying, cry! Let the tears flow. Lift your hands up, bow down on your knees, do whatever you feel, but just don't take your mind off Him. Imagine the cross. Picture how it looks, what it smells like, what it feels like.

Now imagine Jesus being brutally nailed to that cross. Can you see the blood? Can you imagine the pain? Take a deep breath and just pause for a moment. Think about how much He had to love us to endure all that pain. Can you imagine? Are you crying yet?

Well, if not, think about the reason why He came. Think about how He came to earth, knowing what was going to happen to Him. But He came anyway so that He could save us.

We didn't deserve it. We weren't worthy, but He died anyway because He loved us that much. Think about it. Just think about it. Think about how awesome He is, how great He is, and how spectacular He is! Come on, let's worship Him! Tell Him how much we love Him.

Make it personal. Close your eyes tighter and say:

Lord, I love You.

I adore You.

I magnify You.

I worship You.

I exalt You.

I lift up Your holy name.

You are awesome.

You are marvelous.

You are mighty.

The most excellent.

You are a wonderful savior.

You are the forgiver of my sins.

You are the lover of my soul.

The captain of my ship.

The center of my joy.

You are the compassion in my heart.

My redeemer.

My healer.

My companion.

My friend.

My joy.

My help.

My strength.

My refuge.

My vindicator.

My banner.

My provider.

Lord God, You are everything I need.

You are my heart fixer.

My mind regulator.

My peace and my joy.

You are the song in my heart!

You are music to my ears.

You are everything my heart desires.

Lord, I love you!

I appreciate You.

I can't make it without You.

Donyale M. Dabney

I honor You.

I give You glory.

And I bless Your holy name.

I worship You.

I love You.

I thank You.

I thank You, Lord.

I love You.

I love You.

JUST WANNA SAY THANK YOU.

By Donyale Dabney

Verse 1

Jesus, I really love You

And Jesus, I need You too

Without You Lord

Living inside of me

I don't know what I would do.

Jesus, when You gave Your life for me

You saved me

And set me free

Because of You

I am made whole again

Now my life is worth living

So, Jesus, I just wanna say to You

You are my savior; You're my friend.

You're so loving and true.

And yet a comforter too

And I just wanna say thank You

Verse 2

Jesus, my life was all messed up

So much that I

Felt like giving up

Until You shared with me

Your unconditional love

I didn't know what real love was.

Jesus, when I thought

Donyale M. Dabney

I had no one

You said that I

Was a conqueror

I can do all things

In you who strengthens me

Your love is marvelous

(Hook)

So, Jesus, I just wanna say to you

You're my savior; you're my friend.

You're so loving and true.

And yet a comforter too

And I just wanna say thank you

My personal prayer

Father God, in the name of Jesus, I come to You in total submission, making myself available to You. Lord, use me. Use me as a vessel to do your work. Use me to teach your word. Use me to speak your word. Use me to preach your word. Use me to say only the things that you want me to say. Use my mouth to speak truth into your people's lives, Lord. Use my mind to interpret your word, Father. Use my hands to write your word. Use me, Lord, to do all these things so that you would be glorified. Lord, cleanse my heart. Fill me with the power of your Holy Spirit. This is all about you. It's not about me. I surrender my way, my thoughts, my opinions, and I ask you, Lord, that you would usher in your ways, your thoughts, your truth. I decrease right now, asking you, Lord, to increase in me more. Speak to us, Father. My prayer is that your people experience You and not me.

My prayer is that your people hear You and not me. Speak to our hearts. Speak to our spirits and minister unto us. We are open right now to receive your logos word. All these things we ask in your son, Jesus's name, Amen.

Word of The Lord

Setting our foundation

Turn with me if you will **to 2 Corinthians 4:7,** we are going to use this passage as our foundational scripture.

"But we have this treasure in earthen vessels, that the excellency of the power may be of God and not of us."

Let us look at this scripture. What does Paul mean when he says, *'treasure in this earthen vessel?'* Well, before we discuss Paul's intent behind this statement, let's first give a little background on what was going on in this fourth chapter in the hope of shedding some light on the events that led up to this verse. If you do not have your bible, this is probably a good time to go and get it.

For context purposes, let us look at the previous chapters to understand what was going on in that day.

The book of 2 Corinthians begins with Paul addressing certain issues that were going on in the church of Corinth. Paul attempts to obliterate the doubts formed in the people's minds due to his critics using the change in his missionary journey as evidence of him lacking sincerity. In the previous letter to the Corinthians *(ref:1 Corinthians 16:5-7)*, Paul mentioned that he would remain and spend the winter with them. Still, when Paul was unable to follow through, he was not only accused of being unable to keep his word, but they even questioned his Apostleship.

During this time, many false apostles claimed to represent the gospel but were clearly in it for selfish gain. These false apostles opposed Paul and caused much confusion in Corinth. They accused him of being a false teacher teaching unsound doctrine. Paul, of course, addresses these accusations.

In chapter four, Paul begins in the first verse by first expressing, in so many words, the importance of being dedicated, diligent and relentless in preaching the Gospel. Paul felt that because God had chosen him to reveal the gospel's truth and to be a minister of Christ, it would only be right not to give up when things start to get a little rough. Sometimes, when we are challenged with difficulties in our lives, we tend to want to throw in the towel. The Bible says in Galatians 6:9;

"And let us not grow weary in our well doing for in due season we shall reap, if we faint not."

Basically, if we continue running this race, despite any opposition that might come our way, we will, without any doubt, reap everything that God has for us. Paul knew that the church of Corinth would be faced with many challenges during the Christian walk. So, in his own way, he was encouraging them to stay strong and not lose heart.

Oh yeah.... before I go any further, I feel the need to say this.... When studying scripture, we are to understand that all scripture is to be viewed as relevant. Scripture should never be looked upon as 'dead history.' Everything in scripture, old and new, should be interpreted on a personal and prophetic level. Our goal should be to study the history of scripture to learn what God was saying to them then.

Based on what God was saying *then*, we are to take the understanding of that word while keeping it in its proper context and apply it to our lives *now*. When we look at scripture this way, it becomes prophetic. So, all of you out there who are in search of a prophetic word, pick up your bible… read it correctly….and you'll get a word. One that's relevant, personal, and prophetic. hee!-hee! Okay, with that being said, let's get back to the word.

Here, in the second verse, Paul addresses these allegations. In so many words, Paul says that like others that have claimed to teach the gospel but have been guilty of corrupting it in efforts to glorify themselves, he did not take part in this behavior. Withholding the truth and being deceptive to win over or please the hearer was not something he practiced, but rather, he handled the gospel with integrity and sincerity. Paul wanted to clarify to the Corinthians that it was not about what people wanted to hear, nor was it about what made them popular—but was all about the truth. He wanted them to see that the truth of God's word speaks for itself. Nothing should be added, and nothing should be taken away. God does not need us to sprinkle a little on top or, should I say, put a little extra on it in the effort to win someone over. The simple truth of the gospel will do that by itself.

In verses 3 and 4, Paul clearly wanted Corinth to see that if anyone chose not to see or receive the gospel's truth, it was not due to any deceptiveness or embellishment on their part but was instead because they didn't want to. They simply allowed the enemy to blind them from possessing the truth. The enemy or the god with a small "g" of this world's primary goal and mission is to keep the truth away from us. He wants to take as many as he can to hell with him. His ultimate assignment is to do whatever he can to prevent a person from receiving the Gospel of Jesus Christ. He will lie, deceive, manipulate, steal, kill, and destroy to fulfill this assignment.

It is so funny how the enemy will cause people to focus on everything but God. How many times have you spoken to an unbeliever about the Lord, and the first thing he or she says is…? *"Well, you know that all those preachers out there are crooks. All they want is your money… that's why I don't go to church!"* The enemy will take a bad experience or even a bad image of something that relates to God and magnify it to deafen the unbeliever's ears to hear the truth and cloud the unbeliever's eyes from seeing the truth. The enemy knows that if he could point out everything negative, then their eyes will be blinded, as stated in verse 4, *to seeing the gospel of the glory of Christ, who is the image of God.* And if their eyes are blinded, then they cannot receive salvation. WOW! That's deep... If the enemy is blinding the unbeliever's eyes, how do we as believers minister or reach them?

Wow, that's a good question, and it's also a good topic for another sermon. I guess I got to preach on that.... hee! hee! Anyway, I don't have the time to explore that topic right now but getting back to scripture, let's look at verses 5 and 6. Paul says that he and the apostles do not preach themselves, but instead, they preach the message of Jesus Christ. He wanted them to see that they were merely yielded servants to the mission and ministry of Christ. Let's stop and discuss this for a moment. I believe that Paul felt that it was of great importance for him to mention this because back then and even today, we have tended to get so caught up in ourselves and other people that we lose focus on what it's truly about. It is not about us. It is not about the person. I've always said it is not about the Oscar-winning *person* we should follow or focus on, but the Oscar-winning *script*, which is the life-changing Gospel of Jesus Christ. It is the message of the gospel that illuminates our lives. It is the power of the anointing that takes our ordinary lives and makes them extraordinary. It is not us. When Paul mentioned this, he wanted to discourage the people of Corinth from focusing on the lives of him and the apostles. He wanted them to see that they were not anything of themselves but everything in Christ. They have merely mirrored reflections of who Christ was. In other words, they were containers or carriers of His glory; everything that they carried and everything that they held was due to being conformed to the life and example of Christ. That is why Paul says in 2 Corinthians 3:18,

"But we all, with unveiled face, beholding as a mirror the glory of the Lord, as being transformed into the same image from glory to glory, just as by the Spirit of the Lord."

Now let us look at verse 6,

"For God, who commanded the light to shine out of darkness, hath shined in our hearts, to give the light of the knowledge of the glory of God in the face of Jesus Christ."

Paul let us know here that the same God, through His Spirit, revealed to them His attributes and His characteristics through the life of Jesus. The bible says in John 1:14 that the *"Word"* became flesh and dwelt among us, and withheld His glory, the glory as of the only begotten of the Father, full of grace and truth.

So, now that we have walked through each verse, let's go back to our foundational scripture, and maybe we can get a better understanding of what Paul meant by; *"treasure in this earthen vessel."* Let's begin by looking at the word treasure. According to the Webster dictionary, a treasure is of value; something cherished; something adored. A treasure could be money, jewels, gold, or silver. Basically, it is whatever a person deems important to them.

Now let's take a look at the words *"earthen vessel."* What is this earthen vessel? We know that a practical definition of the word vessel is a container. But let's peruse a couple of scriptures in the 10th chapter of Job and then jump forward to the book of 2 Timothy to gain understanding as to what Paul could have been referring to when he mentioned "earthen vessel."

First, let's go to Job 10:8-9.

v-8 "Your hands shaped me and made me. Will you now turn and destroy me? v-9 Remember that you molded me like clay. Will you now turn me to dust again?

We can see here that Job, who was loathing in despair from all he was going through, not only acknowledging that God is responsible for making him and shaping him, but in the "B" portion of verse 9, he poses a question to God that reveals his origin. *"Will you now turn me to dust again?* Although we know this scripture refers to Job, as I stated before, if we make scripture personal and prophetic, the message applies to us as well.

So, in essence, this scripture shows us our origination. It lets us know that we were created from the dust of the earth. Let's quickly turn to Genesis 2: 7 to support what I just said. *"And the Lord God formed man of the dust of the ground and breathed into his nostrils the breath of life; man became a living soul."* We can see in this scripture as well that we were created from the earth. Now let's take a look at 2 Timothy 2:20-21, *"Now in a large house there are not only gold and silver vessels, but also vessels of wood and earthenware, and some to honor and some to dishonor." (V-21) Therefore if a man cleanses himself from these things, he will be a vessel for honor, sanctified, useful to the Master, prepared for every good work."*

In Paul's epistle to Timothy, he strategically paints a picture using analogies to describe the church's current condition. Echoing what Jesus said in the book of Matthew when He spoke of wheat and tares both growing up together, Paul commences making a somewhat similar point as Jesus did. Instead, he refers to man as vessels of gold and silver and vessels of wood and clay, vessels of dishonor, and honor.

Now, based on what we've just read, we know that this earthen vessel that Paul is speaking of is referring to us. So now, with the understanding of the words treasure and earthen vessel, with the context Paul was speaking in the surrounding scripture, it is safe to surmise that in this particular "A" portion of the verse, Paul was merely emphasizing the value and the worth of the gift we have inside us. When we accept Christ in our hearts, we are given a valuable gift. We are no longer considered mediocre, nor do we have to accept operating in mediocrity. We have been given access to the all-powerful knowledge of Jesus Christ through both the principles of His Word and the workings of His Holy Spirit. What does this mean? Well, it is through the word of God we are given the knowledge of who Jesus is, and it is through the workings of the Holy Spirit, we experience who He is.

The Holy Spirit allows the word of God to come alive in our lives. When we yield to the Holy Spirit, we allow Jesus to operate fully in our lives. When we are operating in the world, we are operating in His fullness through the Holy Spirit. Let's take a look at the Holy Spirit related to this treasure that Paul is speaking of.

The Holy Spirit is the third person of the Godhead; God the Father; God the Son; and God the Holy Spirit.

According to the word of God, there are four main functions of the Holy Spirit.

1. He is a "Helper," or "Comforter," which is given to us to help or assist us. *(parakletos)* "*Now, when they bring you to the synagogues and magistrates and authorities, do not worry about how or what you should answer on what you should say. (V-12) For the Holy Spirit will teach you in that very hour what you ought to say.* (Luke 12:11-12) According to John 14:26, He is given to us to teach or reveal to us all things. He will bring back to remembrance what the word has said.

2. He is the "Spirit of Truth," which will lead and guide us into all truth. *(paracletes)* He will teach us the right understanding of the word. The Spirit of Truth vs. the *spirit of error*, according to 1 John 4:5, will help us determine what is of God and what is not. According to John 15:26, the Spirit of Truth is given by the Father, and He will bear witness of Jesus. In other words, He will not speak on His initiative, but only what He hears. He will disclose to us what is to come. He will glorify Jesus and take of His and disclose it to us.

3. He is also given to us to strengthen and fortify us. When we pray in the Spirit, after being baptized in the Holy Ghost with the evidence of speaking in other tongues, we are being built up

spiritually. Jude 1:20 says, *"But ye beloved, building up yourselves on your most holy faith, praying in the Holy Ghost.* The Holy Spirit is there to help us in our weaknesses. According to Romans 8:26, *"For when we do not know what we should pray for as we ought, but the Spirit Himself makes intercession for us with groanings which cannot be uttered."*

4. He is Power, which is given to empower us for service or do His work. The Bible says in Acts 1:8, *"But ye shall be given power after that the Holy Ghost has come upon you: and ye shall be witnesses unto both in Jerusalem and in all Judea and Samaria and unto the uttermost parts of the earth."*

When we embrace or yield to the power and person of the Holy Spirit, we are then given the ability to operate in the gifts of the Holy Spirit. What are the gifts of the Holy Spirit? It is a supernatural means of operating in ways that are beyond our natural abilities.

According to 1 Corinthians 12:4, Paul says that there are diversities of gifts, but the same Spirit. He tells us that there are 9 gifts of the spirit.

Word of Knowledge – Divine knowledge that is downloaded from God's Spirit to our spirit, giving us the ability to know things that we have not learned.

Word of Wisdom – Divine Wisdom is downloaded from God's Spirit to our spirit, giving us the ability to understand things and what to do.

Discerning of Spirits – Divine insight giving us the ability to see beyond the natural into the spiritual realm.

Faith – Divine Faith that gives us the ability to be unhindered by doubt and unbelief. (also referred to as wonder-working faith)

Miracles – Divine intervention in the ordinary course of nature giving us the ability to defy natural laws and abilities.

Healing – Divine healing of sickness and disease without any natural source or means.

Prophecy – Divine utterance in a known tongue gives us the ability to either forth-tell what God is saying or foretell what's to come.

Diversity of Tongues – Divine utterance in an unknown tongue, giving us the ability to speak a message from God. This gift works in conjunction with the gift of interpretation of tongues.

Interpretation of Tongues – A divine understanding and awareness of what has been said in an unknown tongue.

As you can see, there are many benefits of the Holy Spirit, and having attained this wonderful gift, we have truly been given a treasure. I believe that if we yield to this treasure and allow the Spirit of God to flow and comfortably dwell in us, we could truly be effective in this earth's realm.

So, let's take another look at our foundational scripture in hopes of getting a clearer understanding of what is truly being said.

"But we have this treasure in earthen vessels, that the excellency of the power may be of God and not of us."

What is Paul really saying here? Based on what we have learned so far, we know that we, being that earthen vessel, have attained the Holy Spirit that is excellent and of power. If we surrender to the person and power of the Holy Spirit, step out of the way, decrease our vessel, and allow His power to operate, flow, and shine through us, understanding that it is God and not us, then not only will we be used by God, but we will also experience Him in His fullness.

Wow! I can just stop and shout right there. I really don't have to go any further. That is so powerful.... How many of you want to experience God in His fullness? How many of you want to be used by God? I know I would like to. God wants to use us too. He just wants us to be useable, which leads me to what I would like to discuss today. I would like to take this opportunity to talk a little about becoming a useable vessel. In fact, I would like to entitle this message, "Are you a useable vessel?"

Word of The Lord

"Are you a useable vessel?"

What is a useable vessel? Well, we've learned in the previous chapter the spiritual meaning of the word vessel. However, I would like to go a little deeper by exploring the practical meaning.

According to Webster's dictionary, a vessel is a utensil for holding something, like a bowl, kettle, etc. When examining both a bowl and a kettle, we see that, although they were both created with a void, the intent upon creation was for the objects not to remain empty but eventually filled with something. In other words, they were not designed for the mere purpose of themselves but for the substances that would be contained in them. So, to delve a little deeper, a vessel, in so many words, is an empty or hollowed out container or shell made with the express purpose to carry or hold something. Let's take a look at the word 'useable.' We really don't have to go to the dictionary to get a clear definition because all we have to do is break the word down. When we dissect the word, we will see two words: *use* and *able*. Basically, what this word simply means is, being able to be used. So, now when we look at a useable vessel, we can clearly define it as meaning an emptied-out shell with the express purpose of being available and able to be used. I would now like to propose a question. ***Are you a useable vessel?***

Think so? Well, let me propose a few other questions. Are you emptied and able to be used? Are you emptied of all your junk, your intentions, your ideals, your will? Are you willing to let it not be all about you but all about God? Are you willing to be the PR person and not the star? Are you willing to do all the work to promote the star (Jesus) so that His name can go up in big lights and that He can receive all the glory? These are vital questions that you should ask and answer honestly to determine if you meet the requirements of being a useable vessel. As you may already know, there are several requirements you must have to be an effective useable vessel, and, of course, throughout this series, we will be exploring a few of them. However, right now, I want to particularly focus on those things that prevent us from becoming effective useable vessels, those things that hinder us from successfully doing the work of God. Let's take a look.

In my in-depth studies, research, and close observation, I've found that there are several reasons as to why we as Christians have been hindered from the privilege of God's power operating through us. I first began taking an interest in this area when I grew tired of all the disappointing letdowns, regretful mistakes, and held up blessings in my life. I was tired of not experiencing what I knew God had promised me so many years ago. I needed some answers. I needed to know what I was doing, if, in fact, anything to cause these disappointments. In my pursuit of truth, I uncovered some of the reasons I experienced what I was going through. One of the things that I found out was that I was guilty of what I believe is one of the main causes of us not being used by God, and that is, *"Stealing God's glory."*

Are we guilty of stealing God's Glory?

So many times, we find ourselves stealing God's glory. I know you're saying, "Oh no! I would never do that." But, before we go running around thinking that we are holier than thou and Mr. and Mrs. Christian of the year, ladies, let's pull out our compacts, and men, let's stop shaving for a minute and take a closer look in the mirror and a good look at ourselves. Stealing God's glory, what a shame, one might say. I know, when you first hear the statement, stealing God's glory, you may think of it as being something as extreme, such as having the attitude of Satan—basically, trying to take the place of God. However, I've learned from walking this Christian walk that stealing God's glory does not have to be as obvious as Satan's approach but can be done in several small, subtle ways. One way that I've noticed is how we so conveniently take the credit for what God is doing in our lives. How do we take credit from God?

Well, let's examine this for a moment. How many times have you performed or done something in church that was full of the anointing and, as soon as someone complimented you, you said with a haughty look, "Oh thank you," as though it was based on your intellect, talent, or your ability; as though God's anointing had nothing to do with it. And how many times have you thought in your mind or even expressed to others that it was because of you that something was successful? Well, if you have answered this question with a number instead of the word *never*, then you have been guilty of taking God's credit.

Taking God's credit, I know, to some, may seem menial and minute. However, if we are not careful with these trivial areas, the enemy will get us caught up in areas we don't want to be. We must remember that when the enemy attacks us, especially mature Christians, those headed in the direction of being a useable vessel, he does not tempt us with perceptible things. He is most successful when he is subtle. His bait to catch us or draw us outside of God's will isn't with a whole meal. It is with small crumbs planted for us to peck our way right into a direction away from God. That is why we must check our attitudes and ensure that our thoughts and actions align with God's word and not ourselves. Taking the credit for what God is doing is something that God does not and will not tolerate. It is basically going after glory that does not belong to us.

The bible says in Proverbs 25:27;

"It is not good to eat much honey: so for men to search their own glory is not glory."

In other words, it is not good to blow yourself up or toot your own horn. That's slang for *"putting your own name in lights."* When I think of someone operating in this type of behavior, it takes me back to working as a sales administrator at a video duplication company. There was a young lady that I worked with, who I found to be quite hilarious. One day she came to work and was called into the office to meet one of the new executives recently hired. As she sat down in his office, he began to spend time giving her a little background of who he was. As he spoke, she sat there and listened to him go on and on for about half an hour, speaking only of himself. He talked about all the people he had worked with, all his accomplishments, and all his credits. He said, "**I** worked with *this* person, and **I** worked on *this* project, and because of **me,** *this* happened." He said that he had so many credits on his resume that he couldn't even remember them all. She listened for what seemed like forever, and as soon as he finished, she paused and, with the most innocent bright-eyed look, as though she was Penny from the show "Good Times" admiring JJ, she said; **"Wow! You're cool!"** (hee! hee!)

He thought she was impressed with his self-glorification, but in fact, she was merely sarcastic. In other words, what she was really saying was, "Okay, I'll validate you. I'll approve of you."

She recognized right from the beginning that he was fishing for acceptance through self-glorification. Being fully aware of his issue, she gave him exactly what he was looking for, and that was approval.

This type of attitude and conduct is a prime example of how we get caught up in glory stealing. Although this incident may have been secular, so many people in the church today are subject to this same behavior.

I cannot tell you how many times I have sat in churches and listened to people as they, literally, rob God of His glory while sharing their testimony. Instead of giving glory to Him, I've noticed that they will inconspicuously glorify themselves.

For instance, I was visiting a church, and a young girl was giving a testimony about how God used *her*. She said, "*I* was at work, and the Lord sent *me* to speak some words of encouragement." She went on to say, "How *she* said this, and *she* said that, and because of *her* light shining, the woman was drawn to *her*." Then, she went on further to say, "That because *she* was living right, people were able to see the God in *her*, and they could tell that *she* was living saved."

I know you are asking yourselves, what was wrong with what she said? Well, there are a few things wrong. If you look with your 20/20 vision in the spirit and listen closely to a higher frequency in the spirit, you will see that the emphasis was on what *she* did and who *she* was, more so than God. It appears she was in pursuit of giving a self-validation, more so than testifying to the goodness of God. There was more emphasis being placed on her works and not the power within.

We should never emphasize our role in the event; rather, always placing the highlighting on God. We should not testify to the vessel but to the content that's inside the vessel. Have you ever heard of someone coming to a person's home for dinner and, after eating, they complement the pots and pans instead of the meal? I don't think so. That would be total disrespect to the host. So, the same law applies to the Christian walk.

Ephesians 3:20 says,

*"Now unto Him who is able to do exceedingly, abundantly, above all that we could ask or even think of according to the **power that worketh in us.**"*

God does not expect us to showcase our vessels and neglect the power within. In fact, it is the power within that is keeping and sustaining that outward vessel and, without the power, that vessel would be like a puppet without a puppet-master—lifeless.

Wow! I'm ministering to myself right now. I want to move on from this topic, but I am led to continue for some reason. Maybe it's because I'm being set free as I minister this word. This has been an area in my life that I have vowed to pay closer attention to and not fall subject to the enemy's ploys. A lot of us, I have noticed, have been deceived in this area as well, and that is why this needs to be exposed and dealt with. A good piece of information to know is that whenever we find the enemy hanging out in an area of our lives, we must immediately expose him so that he can no longer hide in that area. I have learned that if we keep exposing his hiding places, he won't have any choice but to leave. See, if we don't expose the devil and choose to ignore this problem area in our lives, he will hide out, gain power, and take control, and before you know it, we will end up in bondage and in need of a total and complete deliverance. I've seen this problem slow down and forfeit seasons and hold up destinies. So again, it is so important in this area that we get a proper understanding of how vital it is to let God be God in our lives and give Him all the glory because if we don't, then we can suffer dramatically. I must say, people of God, there is only one King of Kings and one Lord of Lords, and guess what? It is not us. God is the creator of all things who have the power to do all things. God is sovereign, and He is the master behind the plan. He is the driving force behind greatness, and without Him, we are nothing. The bible tells us in Him that we can do all things, but we can do nothing *apart from Him*. When we are connected to the vine, we can bear much fruit, but apart from that vine, we are cast out as a branch that is withered. We need God in everything we do. It is God who has blessed us. It is God who has empowered us and not ourselves. It is not by our might, nor by our power, rather by the Spirit of the Lord.

So, whether giving testimony or giving credit to the source of all things, in seeking vainglory, we are not pleasing God, but instead, we are only pleasing ourselves.

Pride

As I studied and researched how we steal God's glory, one of the questions that kept popping up in my mind was: What type of mindset would cause a person to head in that direction? I learned a long time ago that to deal with problematic areas; we must first identify and expose them by asking ourselves questions that would cause us to examine and confront ourselves honestly. I've also learned that before we can change something, we must challenge it, and before we challenge it, we must confront it.

Confronting our issues, I know, is a very uncomfortable thing to do, but it is vitally necessary for us to overcome them. You see… how can we overcome something that we don't think we have a problem with? How can we get rid of behavior patterns that we are not even admitting exist? We can't! It is impossible, and the devil knows this. He knows that if he could keep us in denial about ourselves, then we will remain outside the will of God, and we would never achieve those wonderful promises of God. The devil's biggest goal is to keep everything God has for us at an unattainable reach. He will even go as far as sending people in our midst to downplay our issues. He'll even send people in our midst to cause us to operate in these dangerous behaviors. So, to confront issues and problematic areas in our lives, we must be honest, and we must ask ourselves those uncomfortable questions. So again, what kind of mindset and thought pattern is it that would have us stealing God's glory? I believe it is a mind that is consumed with pride.

PRIDE…… Wow! What is pride?

Pride is conceit, self-importance, or thinking of yourself a little too much. The Bible says we are not to think of ourselves more than we should or else we'll be deceiving ourselves- meaning we are not to exalt ourselves to a level higher than someone else as though we are better. The Bible also tells us,

"The fear of the Lord is to hate evil. I (which is the Lord speaking) hate pride and arrogance, evil behavior, and perverse speech". (Proverbs 8:13),

"Pride goes before destruction, and a haughty spirit before a fall, (Proverbs 16:18),

"A man's pride will bring him low, But the humble in spirit will retain honor". (Proverbs 29:23),

"But He gives more grace. Therefore, He says: God resists the proud, but gives grace to the humble." (James 4:6),

"Everyone who is proud in heart is abomination to the Lord; Though they join forces, none will go unpunished." (Proverbs 16:5),

"And whoever exalts himself will be abased, and he who humbles himself will be exalted." (Matthew 23:12),

"The pride of your heart has deceived you, you who dwell in the clefts of the rock, whose habitation is high; you who say in your heart, who will bring me down to the ground? (v-4) Though you exalt yourself as high as the eagle, and though you set your nest among the stars, from there, I will bring you down," Say the Lord. (Obadiah 1:3-4).

As we can see, according to the word, pride is something that God hates. Having a heart full of pride is something that God cannot work with. It is something that He will not accept. Why? Because when we are puffed up and full of pride, it is hard for the power of God to operate in our lives. It is hard for God to receive the glory in our lives. We tend to ex God out of the equation, arrogance takes over, and before we know it, we begin praising and worshipping ourselves. It becomes all about us.

Speaking of it *being all about us*, I remember watching the show "Touched by an Angel," which, in my opinion, was one of the best television shows. But anyway, I was watching an episode about a guy who I would say was genuinely a good guy. He was compassionate; He was integral; He was kind and dedicated to his family and employer.

One day while driving home from work, he saw a dog barking on the side of the road, which appeared to have been inadvertently separated from his owner and being the kindhearted guy he was, he pulled over in hopes of reuniting the dog with its owner.

After getting out of his car, the dog led him down a dusty road that led to an old mine. As he entered the mine, he noticed that one of the beams holding up the mine had collapsed, and inside was a woman trapped underneath. Realizing that the mine could fully collapse at any given moment, he called 911, then proceeded to go inside in an attempt to save her. Once inside, the 2nd beam, which was the only support the mine had, collapsed, leaving him with only two options. He could either succumb to being buried alive or attempt to hold the collapsed beam until help arrived. Being determined as he was, of course, he chose to hold the beam.

As he struggled to hold up the beam in the effort to save both his and the injured woman's life, by the grace of God, an angel miraculously appeared to assist him. The woman couldn't believe what she was seeing, but she knew her eyes were not failing her. After seeing this, she assured him that he would be alright because God had sent divine intervention to help him.

Wow! Isn't it funny how God will help carry the load? He is always there, always faithful. This story is amazing; it sort of reminds me of the three Hebrew boys being in the fire. *The king knew he had thrown only three in the pit, but there was a fourth person spotted in the furnace by no surprise. (hallelujah!)*

Anyway, as that third person joined them in the mine, holding up the collapsing beam, he was able to keep the beam from falling for five hours until help arrived. To make a long story short, after the world got wind of his amazing story with no mention of the angel, he had become a hero. Everyone wanted to hear his story. He had become an instant celebrity. He was even given a promotion on his job. Before this heroic event taking place, this man had always felt like no one paid any attention to him. He had always been overlooked and was basically treated like a "nobody." When fame hit him instantaneously, he did not know how to act. The notoriety went straight to his head. It was no longer about the victim that he saved. It was all about him. That kindhearted guy that risked his life to save someone else's had turned into a self-centered, self-absorbed glory hound. He lost himself in all the sudden attention. He was so caught up in his own image he'd stopped helping others, which led him to neglect his job and even his marriage. With this newly developed self-centered, prideful attitude, he ended up losing everything he had.

You see, pride is a dangerous sin. If we are not careful, pride can cause us to lose everything that we have. It can cause us to lose our possessions, friends, family, and even our relationship with God.

Let's take a closer look at this sin of pride. Other than pride being the reason Satan was kicked out of Heaven. Why is the sin of pride so dangerous? Well, let's see. Pride is the only sin that has a long list underneath its covering. What does this mean? Well, I have comprised a list of behavior patterns that describe what a prideful person looks like, and as we peruse this list, we will see that it covers a vast spectrum. Let's take a look:

- **Impatient** - *i.e., "I don't have time for this!"*

- **Quick Tempered** – (Quick to hurt someone's feelings).

- **Judgmental** - (Always pointing out the flaws of others).

- **Easily irritated** - *i.e., "They are getting on **my** nerves!"*

- **Hard time being corrected** - (Justifying everything).

- **Hard time apologizing** - (Saying everything but sorry).

- **Hard time complimenting others** - *i.e., "I don't want her to think she's all that!"*

- **Careless with words** - (Say mean things to others and blame them for being too sensitive when their feelings are hurt.)

- **Arrogant** - (Thinking that they are *all that*.)

- **Entitlement** - *i.e., "I deserved that promotion!"*

- **Self-Righteous** - *i.e., "I don't drink… I don't curse…I don't understand why people do things like that."*

- **Self-Absorbed** - (So concerned with self to the point others are neglected/hurt).

- **Selfish** - *i.e., "It's mine!"*

- **Jealous** - *i.e., "Who does she think she is… she's not all that!"*

- **Competitive** - (Always trying to outdo someone else).

- **Stubborn** - *i.e., "I have made my decision.… I will not yield!"*

- **Never admitting fault** - (Always right and never wrong.)

- **Controlling** - (Nebuchadnezzar Syndrome)

- **Power Abuser**- *i.e., "I did it because I can!"*

- **Enjoy being served but not serving.**

- **Demand respect from others but do not like to give it.**

- **Ungrateful** - (Never say "thank you")

- **Have advice for others but do not like to take it.**

- **Care too much about what you look like to others** - *i.e., "I don't want them to think that I don't have it together!"*

- **Reluctant to ask for help** - *i.e., "I don't want them to think I don't know what I'm doing."*

Those are just a few behavior patterns that I could think of off the top of my head, but the list goes even further than that.

Let me just say this....If you are reading this right now and are saying to yourself, *"Ooo! So and so or such and such should be reading this. This is for them!"* Then you are in pride and thereby need to repent. If God were speaking to them, they would be listening to this sermon right now. But unfortunately, it's not them listening...... it's you. So, in essence, this word is for you.

But on the other hand, perhaps you happened to see yourself while reading this list, don't feel bad. We all have sinned and fallen short of His glory. There is no need to beat yourself up. There's no need to get caught up in condemnation because the bible says, *if we confess our sins, He is faithful and just to forgive us of our sins and to cleanse us of all unrighteousness. (1 John 1:9)* So all you must do is be honest with yourself and repent. In fact, let's do it together because, sadly to say, I saw myself while writing this. So give me your hand....bow your head... and say with me:

"Father God, in the name of Jesus, we humble ourselves before you with a sincere heart, and we repent! We realize, and we confess that we have operated in this forbidden sin of pride, so we ask for your forgiveness. We also ask that you wash us and cleanse us from all unrighteousness in Jesus's name, Amen!

So there you have it! God has forgiven you. All you had to do was ask him. Now with that being said, let's go back to learning more about this sin of pride.

Another thing that I've learned about pride is that once you open the door to this sin, you could very well find yourself committing other sins as well. It has been known as the forerunner or the parent sin of many other sins. It has even been known to cause one to commit murder.

Murder? Wow! How can you say that, Sister Dabney? One might ask. Well, let's go to the word.

Let's look at David's life. I particularly want to take a look at when David sinned with Bathsheba. I know we all know this story as it relates to adultery; however, what I want to do is walk you through this particular event in David's life so that I can point out how this entire act was driven by pride. David's behavior, I believe, is a classic example of how pride can lead a person down a road of committing different sins.

Turn with me to 2 Samuel 11:2-4;

(2) then it happened one evening that David arose from his bed and walked on the roof of the King's house. And from the roof he saw a woman bathing, and the woman was very beautiful to behold. (3) So David sent and inquired about the woman. And someone said, Is this

not Bathsheba, the daughter of Eliam, the wife of Uriah the Hittite? (4) Then David sent messengers, and took her, and she came to him, and he lay with her, for she was cleansed from her impurity; and she returned to her house...

We see here that the scripture shows us that when David first saw Bathsheba, he was taken by her beauty so much that he inquired of her. And although he was informed that she was married, he pursued and sent for her anyway. What does this tell us? Well, it tells me that David, being the King at the time, could have only been thinking of himself and his own desires. It also appears that he could have possibly been guilty of using his power, control, and influence to get what he wanted despite it being morally wrong.

How could you say that Donyale, another might ask? Well, allow me to clarify. I know there have been many interpretations and sermons on this topic, stating that David was tempted through lust, which I've heard in some cases was due to Bathsheba's *calculated seduction.* I've also heard that Bathsheba knew she was married and did not have to lie with the King.

While I respect the interpretation and opinions of others, I beg to differ. Although I love David, and indeed, he was God's man, I do not believe David was the victim here.

For one, he was a man of authority and power who was in the position to do whatever he wanted. He was also a leader who was well respected and often feared. So, with this kind of power and influence, wouldn't you think that it would be safe to surmise that Bathsheba, who was a young woman sitting underneath his rule, could have been intimidated by him and did not feel as though she was in the position to deny his request?

In addition to that, I also must say that I disagree with Bathsheba's *calculated seduction* because, if David had been on the battleground with his army, as a king should have been in those days, he would not have seen her bathing and, therefore, would not have been tempted to begin with. "How about that?" Let's not forget, David inquired of her.

It was not Bathsheba who caused the great King of Israel to fall. His inability to restrain himself from pursuing his selfish desires, *which is considered pride,* caused him to fall.

So, we see here, pride was the initial sin that David was guilty of, and due to him opening that door, he allowed other sins to follow. David then fell into another sin called adultery, and because of this sinful act, he had to suffer many consequences.

Let's go back to 2 Samuel 11:5 and take a look at one of these consequences,

(5) And the woman conceived; so she sent and told David, and said, "I am with child."

Oops! Let's stop and put a pin right there for a moment. I want to deal with this for a second. David, the King of Judah, God's very own, a man after God's own heart, is guilty of pride, adultery, and now having a child with someone else's wife. How does this look for a great King like David to be guilty of this careless act? David knew that he could not let this calamity get out, so what do you think David did? You are absolutely right. He attempted to cover it up. *(and the plot thickens.)*

He sent for Uriah, who was Bathsheba's husband, to come back home from war, hoping that he would lay with his wife so that it would appear as though the child was his. However, Uriah, a faithful and dedicated man, did not feel that it would have been honorable for him to lay with his wife in pleasure while the other servants were engaged in battle.

Oooo! I bet David felt mighty silly. His little plan didn't work. But you see here, this sin of pride now has caused King David to lie and manipulate. Not only has he committed adultery, but he has now become a deceptive liar seeking a way to cover it up. Wow, this sin of pride is no joke! Before you know it, you can be caught up in so many ways. Because David did not want everybody to know that he could make this type of mistake (pride), he chose to cover it up to continue to look good in the eyes of men and found himself digging a deeper hole of destruction.

Although David was in over his head, he did not stop there. David continued to try to cover up this mistake. Let's go back to scripture so that you can read it for yourself. Go down to 2 Samuels 11:14-17;

(14) Then, in the morning, it was so that David wrote a letter to Joab and sent it by the hand of Uriah. (15) And he wrote in the letter, saying; "Set Uriah in the forefront of the hottest battle, and retreat

from him, that he may be struck down and die." (16) Say it happened, while Joab besieged the city, that he assigned Uriah to a place where he knew there were valiant men. (17) Then the men of the city came out and fought with Joab. And some of the people of the servants of David fell; and Uriah the Hittite died also.

Not only did this sin of pride have David committing adultery, with the consequences of having a child out of wedlock, lying, deceiving, and manipulating. But now David has blood on his hands. He is guilty of murder.

So there you have it! We see since David chose to be selfish and do what he wanted to because he felt like it; (pride), he was taken down a road of many sins which, unfortunately, the final destination for him was murder.

Pride in the Church

I know that we have spent a lot of time analyzing pride on an individual level, but right now, I want to spend a little time talking about how pride has affected the church.

Unfortunately, we as believers have allowed pride to creep in and take a standing position in the church, and it has been present for so long that it has even influenced our interpretation of the word. What does this mean? Well, for example, if we look at our modern-day theology in comparison to God's original plan according to the bible, we will see that somewhere down the line, we as the church have adopted a selfish, self-centered, self-absorbed, it's all about me doctrine; and sadly, to say, this has had us for too many years only focusing on ourselves. We have become far more concerned with our personal gain and individuality than we are about elevating as the body of Christ. Instead of uniting together as people of God, we are too consumed with our own advancement in the kingdom. We are too busy trying to benefit ourselves. The bible says in Philippians 2:4 that we are to not only look out for our own interests, but we are also to look out for the interest of others. That is having true concern for someone else. Let's back up and take a look at verse 3 to get a clearer picture. Paul says we should also "Let nothing be done through selfish ambition or conceit, but in lowliness of mind. Meaning- we are to humble ourselves to the point that our concern for others is heartfelt and selfless. In other words, we are to esteem others as being better than ourselves. Wow! That is saying a whole lot. How often do you see this type of interaction in the church? I know, not very often. Instead, we are too busy competing with one another and saying to ourselves as individuals, "how could God bless and prosper me. *My* ministry; *My* destiny; *My* gift; God has anointed *me*. If I might ask, what do all these statements have in common? Well, the one thing I could point out, which is quite obvious, is that they all either start with "*my*" or end with the word or "*me*." I don't know about you, but I was always taught that when the words "I," "Me," and "My" are used in a sentence too often, that is an indication that pride is present.

Pride is such a deadly cancer, and although we can clearly see that this is a common struggle in our church today, this type of selfish behavior has been an issue with God's people for quite some time. However, it was not how God intended for it to be. In fact, right from the beginning, God has always opposed this type of behavior. Let's go to the word and take a look at how God has dealt with this behavior time and time again. Turn with me, if you will, to the book of Joshua and the 7th chapter.

Let me set the stage.... Joshua, who was chosen to lead the children of Israel into seizing the land that God promised to them, learned by God that someone in the camp had taken from the accursed things and had stolen, deceived, and put it among their stuff.

Well, before I go any further, let me first give a little background so that you could get an idea of what was going on.

Joshua and his army, whom the bible says, *"God was with,"* had just succeeded in overtaking Jericho. The bible says in Joshua 6:21, *"and they utterly destroyed all that was in the city, both man and woman, young and old, ox, sheep, and donkey, with the edge of the sword."*

They were well on their way to conquering the land that God had given them until, of course, they came to a small city called Ai.

Ai was a city that was few in number and was considered to be an easy defeat. However, Joshua and his army were morbidly defeated by them and were run completely out of the city.

Joshua, not understanding how this devastating event could have taken place, tore his clothes and fell to the earth on his face before God.

How do you suppose this could have happened if *God was with them*? How could a small city like Ai defeat such an anointed army? Well, as I said earlier, Joshua had learned that someone in his camp had taken from the accursed things. What were the accursed things, and what significance did they have?

Before them attempting to seize Ai, Joshua told the people that the Lord doomed the city to destruction. They were to destroy *everything* leaving *nothing* behind. He said that only Rahab and her family should live. The purpose of this was for them to drive out and get rid of everything that could influence God's people. You see, the land that God had given them was occupied by people who worshipped other gods and who had practices that, if not eliminated, would contaminate the plans that He had for them. In fact, God said in *Joshua 6:18* that the land was under a holy curse. So, in God's eyes, wiping out everything and everybody was not only His way of abolishing any chance of future compromise, but it was also a way to eliminate bringing a curse upon themselves. Indeed, God said, according to *Joshua 6:19*, that the only thing they were supposed to spare was the gold and silver and vessels of iron and bronze. These things were only to be taken to be consecrated as a holy sacrifice unto the Lord. They were to be put into the treasury of the house of the Lord.

As we further read the scripture, we will see that although God gave these instructions, one man disobeyed and secretly kept some of the spoils for himself. This act of disobedience angered God so much that He lifted His anointing, and the entire army lost a battle that they would have otherwise won. Basically, Joshua and his army were held accountable for one man's selfish act.

Wow! This should make us think. Because Achan only thinks of himself, he caused many people to suffer and many to die.

Let's apply this situation to our own lives. I want to know how many of us today, because of our own acts of selfishness, has put other's lives in jeopardy? How many people have we stepped on to get what we wanted? How many livelihoods have we destroyed to reach our goals? When we ask ourselves these types of questions, we expose and challenge who we really are. I believe it is good to take an honest self-evaluation to see exactly where we are and what needs to be dealt with in our lives. If more of us would take the time to do this, we would not only see enormous growth in our lives, but we would also experience a greater walk with God.

If we were to read further on in the scripture, we would see that for the favor to have returned, Joshua had to rectify the problem by first locating and then eliminating the culprit and all that belonged to him. Basically, he killed Achan and his entire family. According to the bible, Achan, all his possessions, and his entire family were taken to the *Valley of Achor*, and they were stoned and set on fire. Wow! because of one man's selfish, self-centered, and only thinking of himself behavior, not only did it cause a lot of people to suffer, but it also cost him and his entire family's life.

So we see here that God never intended for us to be only concerned about ourselves. His original plan and purpose for us were to come together and work towards a common goal to get his work accomplished in this earth's realm. For example, let's look at the early church.

In the book of Acts, particularly the 4th chapter and the 32nd verse, we will see that the people of God were committed to working together. The bible says that *"those that believed were of one heart and one soul."* They were all with one accord, with one agenda. They were so committed to working together that the bible says, *"Neither did anyone say that any of the things he possessed was his own, but they had all things in common." In* God's original plan for the church, there was no room for selfishness. Back then, the people of God were on a mission and serious about doing the work of God. But somehow, in this modern-day walk, it seems as though all that has gotten lost, and we have resorted back to the

Achan way of thinking. We have chosen to follow our own self-centered agendas instead of being obedient to the order that God has already set in place for us. God has a purpose for every one of us, but our purpose is not to benefit ourselves. It is to establish the kingdom on earth as it is already in Heaven. Establishing the kingdom cannot be done by one person. We must unite the body, which comprises many members, infiltrate and influence this world's system.

Before we conclude this topic, I would like to pose a question. *Why are there so many small churches?*........ Well, I believe we have so many storefront churches in our neighborhoods because we have too many people who are willing to be served but not enough willing to serve. Just a little something to make you say, hmmm!

Deliverance From Pride

So far, we have seen how treacherous this sin of pride could be in our individual lives. We have also seen the dangerous effects of this kind of behavior in the church, but what I would like to discuss right now is how pride is developed? Where does pride come from? Well, I've always believed that to confront and deal with any behavior, we must first understand its origination. We must first go to the source by which it arrived. I believe that everything in life has a source. A baby comes from a wound; a plant comes from a seed, and even when evaluating someone's behavior, it is safe to surmise that it has a source as well. In other words, the source is the entrance or the starting place of a particular behavior pattern. This entry is usually caused by a severe emotional wound or injury that has not been dealt with, thereby leaving an opening for the enemy to use that wound to create behaviorisms contrary to Christian beliefs.

So what is the source of pride? Where does pride come from? To answer these questions, let's go back to the word of God. In fact, let's look at David's life again. We learned earlier how David fell subject to the sin of pride, but I particularly would like to take a good look at his childhood this time. I believe that if we carefully examine his childhood, we will see that some of David's negative behavior patterns could have stemmed from the things that happened at the beginning of his life before he became king.

I've found that most behavior patterns, whether good or bad, generally comes from the beginning of a person's life. I believe it is at the beginning where everything is primarily formed. It is where good habits and bad habits are often produced. It is also where certain belief systems are developed. I believe that the beginning is generally the most important part of human development because we are most impressionable and most delicate. It is also where everything is new. I believe when things are new, they are unsullied and most susceptible to influence. For instance, let's look at a new piece of clay.

A new piece of clay, one that is without form or shape and has not had any prior influence, is without question in the best position to take on any shape or pattern. I believe that is how it is with people. When we are young, meaning- when things are still new- is when the enemy tries his best to destroy us. That is where most traumatic wounds and scars are committed. You see, the enemy does not wait until we are adults and ready for ministry to attack us. He starts at birth. He does this because he knows that if he could mess up that perfect piece of clay while it is still fresh, then there may be a chance that that clay will develop with junk, foreign particles, and impurities in it, leaving that once perfect piece of clay, that had the potential to be a masterpiece, into a mold of deformity. The enemy also understands the concept that if he could get us messed up early enough, then there might be a chance that we would spend a lifetime trying to figure out what's wrong with us, which many of us never do, thereby never reaching our destinies. He knows that if he could send certain things our way to hurt or damage us, we would develop certain faults from those experiences, and those faults would keep us in sin, thereby hindering us from walking in purpose.

So, with that being said, let's take a look at the beginning of David's life and try to pinpoint the events that may have caused him to develop certain behavior patterns later on in life.

In the book of I Samuel, particularly the 16th chapter, we see that after Saul was rejected as King, God sent the prophet Samuel to Jesse's house for the mere purpose of anointing the next King of Israel. Jesse, David's father, proudly presented all his sons who were strong in stature except David. Samuel said to Jesse, *"the Lord has not chosen these."* He asked if he had any other sons, then he directed him to David, who was out tending the sheep. Let's stop right here for a moment. As we examine scripture, we see that Jesse did not even consider David as a candidate. In fact, he completely overlooked him until Samuel asked if he had any other sons. Why would a father totally disregard his son? What would make a father eliminate his own son from the lineup of being blessed? In studying the Hebrew scripture, I learned that David was never truly accepted by his father from the very beginning. In fact, he was considered the black sheep of the family. How do we know this? Well, let us look at scripture. I Samuel 16:10-11 says,

> *"Thus, Jesse made seven of his sons pass before Samuel. And Samuel said to Jesse, the Lord has not chosen these. (V-11)*

> *"And Samuel said to Jesse, "Are all the young men here? Then he said, "There remains yet the youngest, and there he is keeping the sheep." And Samuel said to Jesse, "Send and bring him. For we will not sit down till he comes."*

In this text, we not only see Jesse presenting his other sons while David was out tending the sheep, but we also see Jesse referring to David as the youngest. Why is he the youngest important? Being the youngest would have made David the eighth son, and according to I Chronicles 2:13-15, which is a genealogy of the line of Jesse, David was referred to as the seventh son.

Wow! One portion of scripture says he is the eighth son, and another is saying he is the seventh son. How do we reconcile these passages? For we all know that there are no contradictions in the word of God. To resolve this seeming disputation of the text, we must consider the original language of the text. Looking at the word *"youngest"* in Hebrew is the word *"qaton."*

The word *"qaton"* in Hebrew has several meanings. One of the meanings is, of course, being youthful and juvenile as it relates to age. But it also means small, insignificant, reduced, unworthy, least. So, to reconcile this text eliminating all contradictions, the word *"youngest"* used in this text does not mean youthful in age, but it means insignificant; unworthy; least.

David was looked at as the least likely to be considered, the least likely to be chosen. He was considered unworthy and insignificant in his own father's eyes.

Wow! With David being viewed by his father in that manner, how do you suppose this could have affected him? How do you suppose being unaccepted by his father could have made him feel? Well, I believe when Jesse disregarded or should I say overlooked his son. However, it may have appeared inconsequential; this type of behavior coming from his own father could have been devastating to him. It could have perhaps left him feeling neglected, rejected, or even unloved. He could have possibly been made to feel not good enough. When a son feels not good enough in his father's eyes, unfortunately, he is left with insufficiencies that may cause him to spend an entire lifetime having something to prove. Wow! Donyale… that's a little extreme. Let us look at a father's role and how important it is to a son, and then maybe we can see it a little clearer.

A father's role is essential in a young boy's life. He is not only liable for teaching him how to be a man, but he is also the one that instills confidence, security, and strength in him. The father's job is to shape and mold him into what he will be as an adult. He is responsible for validating him, affirming him, and approving him so that he would not have to look to the world to validate him. When a father rejects, neglects, or is just not available physically or emotionally for his child. That child may end up damaged and later develop certain issues, inadequacies, and insecurities that may cause him to act out in ways that may hinder his destiny.

As we clearly see, a father's role is vital to a son. I believe when David's father did not perform his fatherly duties of approving of him in this one instance, and I am sure many other instances throughout his adolescent years, this was the beginning of David experiencing the damaging wound called rejection.

Rejection

***Rejection*....** What is rejection? Rejection is refusing to accept, consider, or recognize. But let's examine further to see how rejection can affect a person's life. Let's look particularly at what one would call *"a wound of rejection."*

A wound of rejection is an offense or injury caused by someone of importance, making another feel unaccepted, unwanted, unworthy, or unloved. Let's peruse down the memory lane of David's life so that we could learn of some of the many things that he went through that could be classified as rejection.

In addition to David's natural father rejecting and neglecting him in his earlier years, Saul, David's father-in-law and could have been considered his spiritual father, later rejected, and mistreated him as well. Let's take a look. The bible says that before David experienced rejection, "*Saul loved David greatly.*" In fact, David was considered his armor-bearer. David served him faithfully by skillfully playing the harp, driving out all evil spirits that tormented Saul. The anointing rested on David as a musician, and when he played, it brought peace to Saul's troubled mind. David was not only a skillful musician, but he was also a mighty man of valor. He was a warrior, and God's hand rested on him. With all these wonderful qualities, David had obviously humbled himself by submitting them to Saul. Why would Saul reject him?

Well, the bible shows us clearly in the book of 1 Samuel that after David prevailed over Goliath and the Philistines, the people of Israel rejoiced and favored him. In fact, if we look at the 16th chapter and particularly the 6th and 7th verses, we will see how all the women came out of the cities of Israel singing and dancing. As they played instruments, the bible says that they sang, "*Saul has slain his thousands and David his ten thousand.*" The people of Israel recognized David's greatness, and when Saul realized this, he grew in hatred and jealousy towards him. He felt his kingship being threatened by all the love David was receiving from the people. He was afraid that David would one day replace his role as King, and due to this, he sought to destroy him. Every chance Saul got, he plotted to kill him, and therefore David spent many years of his life fleeing from the sword of Saul.

So, we see that David received an ongoing rejection from both of his fathers. And although David was not a child during Saul's rejection, due to his submission to him and how he placed himself underneath his authority. I believe it carried the same damaging effect as it did with Jesse.

Let's take a look at what kind of damage rejection may have on a person. I believe when a person experience rejection from a natural or even a spiritual parent, he or she is left with an adverse soul wound that, if not properly ministered to, may, later, affect the mind, will, and emotions. What does this mean? Well, let's look at the way it affects the mind.

A soul wound affects the mind by the way a person thinks. A person suffering from a soul wound is usually bound by unreasonable thought patterns that create certain ideologies that only exist in their head. For instance, they may think that everyone is trying to hurt them, so they lash out in defense, causing harm to other people. I have always said, *"hurt people… hurt people,"* which means - injured people tend to hurt others. When an injured person is suffering from a bleeding wound that has not been healed, they are more likely to react to anything that threatens re-injuring that wound. They will do whatever they feel they have to do to protect themselves, not realizing that the fight is in their own head. The bible says in Proverbs 23:7, *"For as a man thinketh in his heart, so is he."* Meaning - whatever is going on inside a man's thought pattern is usually what he will end up acting out.

In addition to a soul wound affecting the mind, it also affects the emotion by how a person feels. Most people suffering from this wound usually are driven by their emotions, causing them to be extremely sensitive or easily irritated. Whatever they are thinking usually is carried out through their feelings. It is easy to indicate when someone is suffering from a soul wound because they are usually reactive and reckless. Meaning-they do not think or rationalize before they react or speak. Their responses are usually rash and triggered by their temporary sentiments. In addition to that, they often find it hard to be consistent, which in most cases may cause them to live undisciplined and unstructured lives. In other words, *if they don't feel like it, they won't do it.*

This leads me to the final effect of a soul wound. It affects a person's will. When God created us, He did not force us to choose Him or His way but instead, He gave us a gift called *free will.* Free will is the ability to choose our own way or course of action without any restraints. God does not restrain us from choosing Him, but instead, He gives us our own will, which allows us to seek after things that we desire. It is not until we decide to become a believer that we are then expected to surrender or line our desires and our will up with God's will. What is the will of God? Well, the will of God is the Word of God, and as believers, our actions and choices should always reflect the word of God. However, I've learned that when a person is suffering from a soul wound, which causes them to be driven by off-centered thought patterns and impulsive emotions, they usually find it hard to line their will up with the will of God. In other words, they have a hard time doing the word. The bible tells us in James 1:22, *"But be doers of the word, and not hearers only, deceiving yourselves."* He then says further on in verse 25, *"But whoso looketh into the perfect law of liberty, and continueth therein, he is not a forgetful hearer, but a doer of the word, this man shall be blessed in his deeds."* This means that God expects us not just to know His word, but He expects our lives to replicate His word, and in doing so, we would be blessed. So, we see this condition could not only cause an enormous amount of hurt and pain but, if not dealt with, it also could prevent us from being blessed.

This wound of rejection is an extremely dangerous offense, and it is not something that should be overlooked. I know many of us tend to think that repressing and sweeping those hurtful experiences in childhood under the rug could make it all go away. However, if the truth be told, when we allow things to go unresolved for too long, we run the risk of making matters even worst. I've always said that it is likened to a small scrape that has gone untreated. Eventually, that scrape will develop an infection, and if still not treated, gangrene will set in. Wow! I know that that may have been a bit graphic. But we must understand the serious ramifications of ignoring our issues. If they are not dealt with, they could destroy us.

Let's take a look at some indicators of how we know if we are dealing with the wound of rejection:

- **Hide behind a façade (Fake)** - *afraid to reveal their true self in fear of being not accepted.*

- **Hard time being honest** - *tell people what they want to hear.*

- **Lack of trust** - *questioning everything and everyone.*

- **Extremely guarded** - *not giving people access to you. Push everyone away.*

- **Low Self-Esteem** - *extremely insecure.*

- **Fears of Expectation** - *An extreme fear of being let down.*

- **Strong need for attention** - *want to be seen.*

- **Strong need for approval** - *seeking validation.*

- **Strong need for acceptance** - *seeking the praise of men.*

- **Hard on themselves** - *Unrealistic need to be perfect. (Perfectionist).*

- **Extremely sensitive** - *touchy and easily offended.*

- **Hard time in intimate relationships** - *clingy/obsessive*

- **Hard to get along with** - *sabotage relationships; hurt them before they hurt you. Leave them before they leave you.*

- **Sabotage themselves** - *deliberately destroy opportunities and potential blessings in fear of being disappointed.*

- **Introverted** - *Have extreme difficulty communicating and expressing feelings.*

- **Inferiority issues** - *Easily intimidated, seeing themselves as lower in value and quality than another.*

- **Victim mentality** - *Thinks everyone is against them.*

- **Nonchalant** - *"I don't care!"*

- **Passive** - *"Saying yes to everything." Difficulties setting boundaries.*

As I said before, if you happen to see yourself, don't get discouraged. It is never too late to get it right. God is a God of restoration. He is a God that will take what we consider to be ruined and rebuild. He delights in taking something lifeless and pouring His power into it and resurrecting it back from the dead. He is truly awesome.

So, with that being said, how do we deal with rejection? How do we counter rejection? How do we get rid of it?

Let's look at how David handled his rejection, and maybe we could learn how to overcome this issue.

Looking at David's life, I believe he eventually dealt with and overcame this condition by drawing closer to God. According to scripture, David opened himself up to his Heavenly Father and received the unconditional love that was available to him. When he felt he had no one, he trusted God to strengthen and restore him. He wrote in Psalms 18:2-3,6,19

"The Lord is my rock, and my fortress, and my deliverer; my God, my strength, in whom I will trust; my buckler, and the horn of my salvation, and my high tower. v-3 I will call upon the Lord, who is worthy to be praised: so, shall I be saved from mine enemies."

v-6 "In my distress, I called upon the Lord and cried unto my God: he heard my voice out of his temple, and my cry came before him, even into his ears."

v-19 "He brought me forth also into a large place; he delivered me because he delighted in me."

I believe that sometimes we go through things in life for us to draw closer to God. When man rejects us, God is always there. In fact, he says in His word that He will never leave or forsake us. God is always available to us. He is faithful. 1 Corinthians 1:9 says, *"God is faithful, through whom you were called into fellowship with His Son, Jesus Christ, our Lord."* He will never reject us. He will never throw us away. It says in Ephesians 1:4,

"just as He chose us in Him before the foundation of the world, that we should be holy and blameless before Him in love." He also says in 1 Peter 2:9,

"but you are a chosen race, a royal priesthood, a holy nation, a people for God's own possession, that you may proclaim the excellencies of Him who has called you out of darkness into His marvelous light." As we see, according to scripture, we are chosen by God. He

validates us and reaffirms us throughout scripture, so it would behoove us not to draw closer to thee. In David's case, we know that his rejection manifested in the form of pride. Still, because of the time David spent with his Heavenly Father, I believe he could receive the therapy he needed to overcome his issues to have a successful life. Yes, David may have messed up and fallen into sin with Bathsheba, but because he loved God and had a personal relationship with Him, I believe David overcame those things that haunted him in his past. He was able to go to his father in Psalms 51 and say,

V-1 "Have mercy upon me, O God, according to thy lovingkindness: according unto the multitude of thy tender mercies blot out my transgressions. V-2 Wash me thoroughly from mine iniquity, and cleanse me from my sin. V-3 For I acknowledge my transgressions: and my sin is ever before me. V-4 Against thee, thee only have I sinned and done this evil in thy sight: that thou mightest be justified when thou speakest and be clear when thou judgest. V-5 Behold, I was shaped in iniquity; and in sin did my mother conceive me. V-6 Behold, thou desirest truth in the inward parts: and in the hidden part thou shalt make me to know wisdom. V-7 Purge me with hyssop, and I shall be clean: wash me and I shall be whiter than snow. V-8 Make me to hear joy and gladness; that the bones which thou hast broken may rejoice. V-9 Hide thy face from my sins and blot out my iniquities. V-10 Create in me a clean heart, O God; and renew a right spirit within me. V-11 Cast me not away from thy presence; and take not thy holy spirit from me. V-12 Restore unto me the joy of thy salvation; and uphold me with thy free spirit. V-13 Then will I teach transgressors thy ways; and sinners shall be converted unto thee. V-14 Deliver me from blood guiltiness, O God, thou God of my salvation: and my tongue shall sing aloud of thy righteousness. V-15 O Lord open thou my lips; and my mouth shall shew forth thy praise. V-16 For thou desirest not sacrifice; else would I give it: thou delightest not in burnt offering. V-17 The sacrifices of God are a broken spirit: a broken and a contrite heart, O God, thou wilt not despise. V-18 Do good in thy good pleasure unto Zion: build thou the walls of Jerusalem. V-19 Then shalt thou be pleased with the sacrifices of righteousness, with burnt offering and whole burnt offering: then shall they offer bullocks upon thine altar.

So how did David overcome pride? Well, according to this passage of scripture, he first humbled himself by repenting. He admitted that he had issues. He admitted that he was messed up, and he realized he couldn't fix his problems himself. He understood that it would take a merciful God full of love and compassion to correct those things he was dealing with. After his admission to guilt, he then opened himself up to God, giving Him access to the cracks and crevices of those hidden parts of his heart. He knew that the power of God could only remove the damage that was done in his life. God was the only one who could heal the core of his defective soul.

With that being said, if we truly want to overcome this pride issue, we must do what David did and go back to the beginning. We must deal with the core. We must move past the fault and deal with the need. I believe once we locate that need and fix it, the bondage of our fault will be severed, and then we will be truly set free.

Let's pray,

"Father God, in the name of Jesus, we realize that you understand the complexity of every issue we deal with. We also know that you are God that looks beyond our faults and see the need.

Lord God, we recognize that you are the ultimate physician; the Divine therapist who is able to do exceedingly, abundantly, above all that we could ask or think according to the power that works in us. You can heal any wound, great or small. In fact, your word says in Isaiah 53:5, *"you were wounded for our transgressions, you were bruised for our iniquities. The chastisement of our peace was upon you and by your stripes we are healed."* That means your healing is available for every sickness, every disease, every physical wound, and every emotional wound. It is even available for this nasty wound of rejection. All we have to do is ask. Your word says that if we ask, it shall be given; if we seek, we shall find. If we knock, the door shall be open unto us. Lord God, we ask that you heal the very core of us. Heal the little girl/boy in us. Heal the adolescent in us. Heal the teenager in us. Heal the young man/woman in us. Now heal the grown man/woman in us. Heal every broken part of us, Lord. Let your healing virtue mend every shattered piece of us so that we could operate in your fullness. Devil, we take authority over you. You no longer have access to our pain. You can no longer use our hurt against us. We forgive everyone that has ever rejected us in our childhood. (*name every person*) We declare that this ailment of rejection no longer binds us, but we are complete, whole, and healed in Jesus mighty name."

If you have prayed this prayer with all sincerity and believe that you have received, then you are truly set free. We have reversed what the devil meant for evil through our prayer of agreement and turned it around for our good. No longer will we be held back by our damaging past, but like David, God is going to take all the hurtful rejection and use it for His glory. If you truly believe this, somebody says Amen!

We are going to stop right here for now. We will pick back up on this topic in part II of the series *"Are you a useable vessel?"* in hopes of tackling it in its entirety. So far, we have learned what a useable vessel is. We also have pointed out some of the key things that may hinder us from becoming an effective useable vessel. I have been blessed, and I'm sure you have been blessed as well. However, the time has come now where I must extend the invitation to accept Christ as your Lord and Savior. If you have not accepted Christ as your Lord and Savior, then now is the opportunity to do so. You do not have to be in a church institution to do it. You can do it right where you are. This commitment is between you and God. That is why it is called *"Personal Savior."* I will walk you through the process, which is quite simple, and I'll give you some foundational scriptures for your understanding.

Altar Call

The Bible says in **John 3:16**, *"For God so loved the world that He gave His only begotten Son, that whoever <u>believes</u> in Him should not perish but have everlasting life."*

So, what does this mean? Well, let me give you a brief background. In the beginning, when God created Adam and Eve (which represented mankind), He gave them a direct command, and He told them not to eat from the tree of good and evil and instead of them listening to God's command, they disobeyed Him. (*this is the accelerated version, so I'm not going to get into detail*) Because of their disobedience, sin was let into the world and mankind not only died spiritually but they were separated from God. So, what does this mean? Well, when God created mankind, **we (All)** were connected to Him, but when mankind disobeyed, **we (ALL)** were separated, and we became sinners. Because of this act, everyone who was born into this world (black, white, Hispanic, green or blue) automatically became a sinner. Before I go any further, let me first define sinner and then explain the consequences of being one. A sinner is someone who chooses to live a life disobedient to God's word and the wages, which is the payment of sin is death.

Oh, but I am a good person, I know one might say………

But the bible's response to that is **Romans 3:10**, "There *is none righteous, no not one.*" The bible also says in **Romans 3:23**, "for *all have sinned and fall short of the glory of God.*"

What does this mean? Well, this means that it really does not matter how good you are or how many homeless people you gave a dollar to; without Christ, you are still considered unrighteous or a sinner.

Well, the bible says in **2 Corinthians 5:21**, "For *He (God the Father) made Him (Jesus) who knew no sin to be sin for us, that we might become the righteousness of God in Him.*

Oh wow! That sounds like hope. One would say.... Well, Jesus, who knew no sin, took upon Himself the sins of the world and died in our place. So, because He did this, we were given the opportunity to change our sinner/unrighteous status through Him.

You see, God did not give up on us because He loves us. He says in **Romans 5:8,** "*But God demonstrates His own love towards us, in that while we were still sinners, Christ died for us.*"

You see, God sent us a Savior to save us from the destruction that disobedience led us to. So how do we change our unrighteous/sinner status through Him? How do we become saved?

Well, I'd thought you'd never ask. **Romans 10:9 says,** "*that if you confess with your mouth, the Lord Jesus and believe in your heart that God raised Him from the dead, you will be saved.*" If we continue reading the next verse, it gives us an explanation. **v-10** "For *with the heart one believes to righteousness, and with the mouth confession is made to salvation.*

So now that I've given you a brief explanation as to what? Why? And how? If you are interested, let me walk through the steps to salvation.

Repeat after me. (Speak it sincerely from your heart)

Dear Heavenly Father,
I admit that I am a sinner,
And I need a savior,
I realize that I have been living a life separated from you, and
I am sorry,
I ask Lord God that you save me,
I believe that You have sent your son Jesus on earth and He died for me on the cross, and His blood was shed for my sins,
I also believe that He was buried.
and on that third day, He rose,
I confess you, Lord Jesus, right now as the <u>Lord</u> and <u>Savior of my life.</u>
And I also ask that You fill me with the power of the Holy Spirit.

Thank You, Lord, for loving me enough to not give up on me but making salvation available to me through Your son, Jesus! Amen.

So, there You have it. If You have prayed this prayer, You are no longer separated from Christ, and You now have everlasting life. You are no longer considered a sinner!!! Praise God. You just don't know how happy You have made God. The angels are rejoicing in heaven right now because of the decision you have made. I praise God for you, and I pray that God will reveal Himself to You through His Holy Spirit so that You will get to know Him in His fullness. I pray blessings and favor on Your lives, and I pray that it will not stop here, but God will lead you to a good church so that you will learn the word and grow. I thank you, Heavenly Father, for the souls that will be saved by way of this book.

Study Notes

Study Notes

Study Notes

Study Notes

Study Notes

Study Notes

Acknowledgements

My special thanks to my beautiful daughters, Meagan Jenne Alexander-Underwood and Cameryn Kennedy Rabb, for sharing their mother with Destiny. I also want to thank my handsome grandson Cayden for being such an inspiration. My thanks and appreciation to my beloved pastor Dr. Michelle Corral who has been my teacher; my preacher; my personal destiny coach; and my spiritual mom all wrapped in one. I could not have summoned the courage to keep going without your love and support. I dedicate this project to my Auntie Glenda. There aren't any words to describe how much I love and appreciate you. I'm getting choked up while writing this.... Truly I don't know what to say. You stepped in when I was going through the most difficult time in my life. You supported me when I didn't know what I was going to do. I thank God for you. I thank God for your sacrifice, for your love and obedience to Him. I pray that God would bless me just so I can buy you the biggest mansion in the world and give you back all the things you gave me. I thank you so much! Thanks to all my family and friends. I love you all!

About The Author

Apostle **Donyale M. Dabney** is an anointed woman of God. Born in Oakland, California, she is a devoted mother of two beautiful daughters Meagan and Cameryn: and a handsome grandson Cayden. She is a visionary, true worshipper, intercessor, prayer warrior, author, singer/songwriter, ordained prophet, and an anointed teacher of the Gospel who loves God and His word.

Apostle Donyale, through her hunger for the deeper things in scripture, sat at the feet of Dr. Michelle Corral and studied Torah for 14 years. This intense study not only has increased her knowledge of the Hebrew scripture but has also shaped her into having an impeccable Godly character. Her studies of *Musar*, which is the study of ethical and moral discipline, have been engrafted into the very foundation of her ministry. It has influenced her teaching in a way that promotes integrity and holiness. Her in-depth studies of the New Testament scripture from a Hebraic perspective further developed her hunger which ultimately led her to receive a Master's in Hebraic Based Biblical Studies at Melodyland School of Theology.

Apostle Donyale faithfully served many years as a personal intercessor and armor bearer to Dr. Corral and travelled internationally to Dubai and Indonesia, ministering in revivals and healing crusades. She served as a prayer coordinator and prophet in Breath of the Spirit Ministries and Head of intercession for the Antelope Valley Unity Tent Revival in Lancaster, California, and she has served her community through partnering with various organizations in providing the homeless hot Thanksgiving meals annually.

Apostle Donyale is the Founder of **Testimony Times International Ministries** *and* **Gathering of the Remnants Prophetic Bible Study**. *She is the Founder of* **5AM Gathering Prayer Ministry** *and* **Bread of Heaven Outreach**. *She is the author of four books,* **"Let's Detox the Soul Prayer Manual/CD, Let's Have Church/Are you a useable Vessel,"** *and* **Let's Gather Together in Prayer/Deliverance for Destiny**. *She is also the CEO of* **The Billy Sue Company/Billie Sue Designs**, **Billie Sue Products**, *and* **Billie 2 Billy Music/Publishing**.

Apostle Donyale is a Kingdom-minded dedicated useable vessel. She has committed, surrendered, and consecrated her life to serving the Kingdom of God in every way she can. Through her ministry of love, compassion, and mercy, she has drawn many to Christ. Through her natural transparency and humor, God has strategically used her as an example and a light to not only lead many to Christ but also to influence those who have backslide in faith to recommit their lives back to Him.

Apostle Donyale knows all too well what it means to struggle. Throughout her journey and many years of tears, trials and struggles, God has taken her pain and turned it into gain by giving her tools, skill and understanding; and unique methods of presenting the Word in such a way that presents Jesus as our Divine Therapist. This method has been effective in bringing forth healing, deliverance, wholeness and ultimately transformation, purpose, and destiny not only in her life but also in the lives of others. God has richly blessed prophetess and through His Grace, He is blessing others through her ministry.

OTHER BOOKS WRITTEN BY AUTHOR

WHAT IS DETOXING THE SOUL?

Detoxing the Soul is getting rid of all the deadly toxins, poisons, impurities, and filth that lie in the core of our soul. Caused by hurts, pain, disappointments, and traumatic experiences, these toxins are released when issues have not been properly dealt with; when things like verbal abuse, sexual abuse, and physical abuse have not been addressed. We know when things are hidden and swept under the rug and not exposed, they can cause severe damage to our soul. During the course of this CD you will experience a supernatural healing and breakthrough in your soul that only the Anointing of God can do. Your mind will be renewed; your heart will be purified; your emotions will be healed and made whole so that ultimately your 'Will' will line up with the Will of God. So are you ready to be healed, set free and delivered. Are you ready for the chains to be broken off? Well, let us go before the throne of Grace and ... **DETOX YOUR SOUL.**

OTHER BOOKS WRITTEN BY AUTHOR

Deliverance for Destiny is a strategic prayer that allows you to cry out to God for deliverance... for freedom... and liberty.

This prayer allows you to cry out for Him to break off the chains and everything that has had you bound...everything that has been stopping you from thrusting forward.

Through the authority that God has given you and the power of the blood.... the blood of the lamb (Exodus 12), every demonic force, every diabolical assignment, and every Spirit of Pharaoh will have to release you and let you go!

To Schedule Apostle Donyale Dabney at your church, conference, or special event, email us: testimonytimesim@gmail.com

ADDITIONAL MATERIAL ONLINE FOR APOSTLE DONYALE M. DABNEY WWW.TTIM.ORG

www.ingramcontent.com/pod-product-compliance
Lightning Source LLC
LaVergne TN
LVHW091556060526
838200LV00036B/866